BOA
EDITIONS LTD

DÍWATA

DÍWATA

POEMS BY
BARBARA JANE REYES

AMERICAN POETS CONTINUUM SERIES, No. 123

BOA EDITIONS, LTD. ☐ ROCHESTER, NY ☐ 2010

First Edition
10 11 12 13   7 6 5 4 3 2 1

For information about permission to reuse any material from this book please contact
The Permissions Company at www.permissionscompany.com or e-mail permdude@
eclipse.net.

Publications by BOA Editions, Ltd.—a not-for-profit corporation under section 501 (c) (3)
of the United States Internal Revenue Code—are made possible with funds from a variety
of sources, including public funds from the New York State Council on the Arts, a state
agency; the Literature Program of the National Endowment for the Arts; the County of
Monroe, NY; the Lannan Foundation for support of the Lannan Translations Selection
Series; the Sonia Raiziss Giop Charitable Foundation; the Mary S. Mulligan Charitable
Trust; the Rochester Area Community Foundation; the Arts & Cultural Council for Greater
Rochester; the Steeple-Jack Fund; the Ames-Amzalak Memorial Trust in memory of Henry
Ames, Semon Amzalak and Dan Amzalak; and contributions from many individuals na-
tionwide. See Colophon on page 84 for special individual acknowledgments.

Cover Design: Sandy Knight
Cover Art: "Masamang balita galing sa mga bituin" by Christian Cabuay
Interior Design and Composition: Richard Foerster
Manufacturing: Thomson-Shore
BOA Logo: Mirko

Library of Congress Cataloging-in-Publication Data

Reyes, Barbara Jane.
  Diwata / by Barbara Jane Reyes. —1st ed.
     p. cm.
  ISBN 978-1-934414-37-8 (alk. paper)
  I. Title.
  PS3618.E938D59 2010
  811'.6—dc22
                          2010009192

BOA Editions, Ltd.
250 North Goodman Street, Suite 306
Rochester, NY 14607
www.boaeditions.org
A. Poulin, Jr., Founder (1938–1996)

NATIONAL
ENDOWMENT
FOR THE ARTS
A great nation
deserves great art.

State of the Arts
NYSCA

Contents

For Tita Alice Pulmano
1939–2006
Storyteller, Spirit

For Eustaquio Garcia Pulmano, MD
1912–2007
Monument, My Papa

"Pic, pic, pic, tic, tic, tic, Look thou god of the air and lord of the birds. With only a peck of thy strong beak thou wilt give us freedom. Thou wilt be joyful at seeing us, and we shall thank thee with all our hearts."

The sound came from the bamboo reed—persuasive and distinct. "Should I peck on the reed?" the cautious Manaul hesitated. At that very moment, the bird thought he saw a lizard scamper up the reed. Suddenly, as a reflex action, he jumped and pecked hard.

The bamboo cracked and slowly split open. Lo and behold, the first man and the first woman sprang from inside the hollow space of the bamboo node!

Sicalác, the male, was strong and handsome and was named Malakás, meaning strong. Sicabáy, the female, was beautiful and lovely and was named Magandá, meaning beautiful. Since then, men were called si Lalác or lalake, and women were called si Babay or babae.

—Penélope V. Flores, "Malakás at Magandá"

◻

And the Lord God caused a deep sleep to fall upon Adam, and he slept: and he took one of his ribs, and closed up the flesh instead thereof;

And the rib, which the Lord God had taken from man, made he a woman, and brought her unto the man.

And Adam said, this is now bone of my bones, and flesh of my flesh: she shall be called Woman, because she was taken out of Man.

Therefore shall a man leave his father and his mother, and shall cleave unto his wife: and they shall be one flesh.

—Genesis 2:21–24

A Genesis of We, Cleaved

In the beginning, a man of dust and fire became bone, and viscera, and flesh. The deity of the wind blessed his lips, and he came to take his first breath. Within this strange vessel, I opened my eyes, and within this, your darkness, I learned to weave song. Do you remember me fluttering inside your chest, tickled by the cool air newly filling your lungs? Do you remember exhaling song on this first day?

On the second day, the unseen hand from above cleaved you in two, exacting penance for our joy as you awakened from the deepest, most delicious dreaming. On the second day, my love, I was torn from the haven of your blood, the cradle of your flesh and tendons. A smarting wound strewn across our garden's sweet grasses, I lay raw and aching. On this second day, my hands and feet learned how relentless the cold.

On the third day, I found river, and plunged the wisp of my body into its current. As I learned to breathe without you, as I mimicked the river's lullaby, you appeared upon its banks, your body so fissured, your eyes the ravaged jewels of an umber earth. There were no words for the sorrow bolting through me then, as I watched your hands touch the scarring place where I began. On this third day, my mirror, we learned lamentation, and shadow.

On the fourth day, I sang a dirge, the river my harmony. From afar, you watched me, as the unseen hand from above offered you reparations for your brokenness. More than anything, I thirsted to embrace you in our ocean, for its saltwater to heal us both. But my mirror, the memory of your darkness welled up inside me every time I drew near. On this fourth day, I learned to weep. On this fourth day, the scars hardened over your heart.

On the fifth day, I dreamed such fire, the birth of suns and thunder. I dreamed this garden, reduced to ash. I dreamed that from loss, we began again, a we that knew only of being whole, of sharing heart, and breath, and salt. A feast of we, luminous as the secret of fruit and seed. A we impervious to cleaving, to fracture. On this fifth day, I opened my eyes and I came to know of hope.

On the sixth day, I came to you, and told you of this dream. I touched your scars. You whispered a prayer. I gave you my secrets. You gave me your words. I asked for your breath. You gave me your seed. And as our bodies folded into each other, we dreamed the same honeyed light. Upon awakening, you named me for the morning. But on this sixth day, the unseen hand from above wrested you from me, cleaved us in two once again, and weighted the heaviest sorrow upon me. Never once did he show himself.

On the seventh day, my love, I surrendered.

THE BAMBOO'S INSOMNIA

I can't sleep. There is a poet stuck between the love lines of my palms. And I would tell her to get out if I could, but there is a poet stuck inside the cradle of my bones and tendons.

Diwata

I.

There once lived a strange deity who was only strange because few strove to know her. *¡Bárbara! ¡Que barbaridad!* taunted her eldest brother, who was lightning. Her own light was confined to a glass vial. She knew stars an ascension of pearls hung by Gigante on the highest tree boughs. When he danced, earth descended beneath his feet. There below, a vain woman, earthbound. She knew tongues of many men, those who brought boats and steel, those who brought silks and jade, those who brought the cross.

But this story lacks proper symmetry.

A woman's hands make fine threads dance. With needles of carabao horn, of bamboo, she embroiders names into silk—serpent ulap scale luna fire lihim gem azul eye liwanag river mariposa light talà—when she weaves these words into the fabric of sky, a charm against forgetting. With ink and thread she draws her own hands *pero siempre estas manos desaparecen*; she weaves enkanto contra palabras vaporosas, poemas contra vacía alma. And when her face begins to resemble the porcelain virgin's face, for this firelight causes much to appear, still she sings: *o diwata, your words are our breath! O diwata, our words are our offering to you!*

2.

Some say thunder, child of the earth, calls to lightning, child of the sky, because they are twins, split in two by their spirit father. As the mortal woman ascended with her lover, the path through clouds to sun burned. Her flesh also burned. The child below the villagers wished to keep, so that the spirit father would always return to them.

Yes, he cleaved his son in two. And from these halves, the one skybound grew a new self just as the butiki who's lost his tail. The one below would have perished had not the spirit father descended and breathed his breath into the lifeless half body. This one, how his voice booms when his twin brother streaks across heaven.

And their sister, the strange diwata whose light remains contained. Witness she is, and weaver. If she would only speak, then she would tell you—*these stories I give you, I swear they are the truth.*

3.

Before this time, sky was high as a tent. Children poked clouds with bamboo sticks. Some could jump high enough to touch it with their fingertips. When headhunters danced around the bonfire, keeping vigil, their blades pierced the skins of the gods.

. . .Yes, hija, we were headhunters once, our people. . .

There, the battlefield between forest and river's edge, littered with headless bodies. The heads they took to their own village for they believed the soul resided there. Beyond the distant lowlands, a deity whose winged head our god buried with the remains of the serpent who ruled the clouds. The orphan spirit, whose body our god set afire. This is how he invited his enemy's soul to be his spirit guardian.

Some also say, this was how the first coconut tree came to grow.

4.

Once a diwata stole fire. He brought it to the riverbanks where the earthdiver
shivered, unclothed. This was her fate for peering through the hole in the
clouds while her father hunted the red deer and the wild boar. She had
grown tired of animal bones scattered, a house of musk and taut skins.
How she'd wince as her father's sharpened teeth pierced his prey's liver.

There is no secret in fire, the diwata told her years later, after they had wed,
after the ocean floor's black mud bubbled to the surface, birthing islands.
Others say the maya bird taunted sky, and ocean revealed its hidden contents
in epic warfare. But the earthdiver remembers it this way: mighty Lawin
dropped her upon the back of the eldest tortoise. Masqueraded as dove,
Lawin cooed, *Paloma, paloma, dalagang paloma! Amorcita paloma, minamahal kita,
paloma!* He took her there, he gave her child. She fled deep into the glowing
darkness of salt caves, where the virgin draped in sky wept silver tears. She
taught young village girls to guard its entrance and wail. *O diwata, kaawaan
po ninyo ako!* But he pursued, captured her. *Dalaga, dalaga, dadagitin kita, dalaga!*
A tent of skins and tools carved of animal bones, these were her dowry.

5.

He took me, from my hole in the clouds. He took me, gripped between his talons. I feared that if I tried to escape, I would fall into the deepest, the bluest ocean. I knew for sure I would drown, for I had lived my entire life in my father's realm and had never before touched water. When mighty Lawin came with his sugared words, I leaned farther over the edge than I should have. But so pretty, his words. Upon the shell-mound of kind Pawikan, there, Lawin took me and took me, and Pawikan could do nothing. I knew my brothers too would do nothing. There, he tore me in two.

My child, your father's eyes. My child, one day you will fly.

6.

The child tore at his mother's breast for he was born with talons and a tendency towards treetops. When he grew old enough to climb, he built a nest in the knotted, ancient tree and refused to descend despite his mother's calls, despite her tears.

She brought the child rice wrapped in banana leaves. She whispered, *tabi-tabi po*, to the air around her. She bowed as she approached the tree's giant roots which forced up earth and made caves. Ants and the anito lived in these. Everyday she did this. She feared he would starve, but the spirits of the tree taught him to lure and snare bee-eaters, flame-breasted doves. *Kalapati, kalapati! Kalapati, kalapati!* He'd sing and coo; he'd cradle sunbirds in his claws and then crush their fine bones.

A season ago, hunters' arrows felled mighty Lawin. After this, she lived alone. She dreamed his plumage adorned elders' headdresses by firelight. How they'd bare their blackened teeth. How these with the blackest teeth were most beautiful. How she never returned to her father's realm.

7.

On the darkest nights, some say a tree spirit takes off her wings to bathe in the forest lake, and her wings the hunter hides in the heart of mangrove thickets. No ancient forest spirit he is, but a man. In the wet earth, tracks like no other, and no scent. Because he is a hunter, he lures her to his village home. Because she is diwata, she feigns capture. For his every kill, the elders have marked his skin with glyphs resembling reptile scales, owls' eyes, thunderbolts. Sunbursts and daggers along his arms' sinews. And one day, perhaps today, to be inscribed where the rib cage opens, a circle broken, pointing upwards to its own center. Hanging from his earlobes, this same symbol, carved of carabao horn, washed in the animal's blood.

The old ones say when he hides her wings, she sits upon a rock and weeps. He clothes her in a gown of tree bark. He warms her body with his own. He teaches her to weave dancing women, leaf storms, rice terraces into midnight colored cloth. The old ones say she uses human hair to bind mother of pearl shells to boars' teeth, and human skulls to doorposts.

. . .Yes, hija, our people, once headhunters. . .

8.

I am the tree, and thinking me naked, he blankets me in a dress of my own skin. Upon my head, a wreath he's weaved from the leaves and branches of my own crown. This death shroud for the living, though he believes himself to be kind-hearted in this gesture. His arms are sturdy from hewing down many of my kin, and his body smells of the animals whose lives he takes. I could flay him, and fashion a musky death shroud of his skin. But when he comes to me, mute, clothed in the scent of the dying, and seeking passage through my thickets—tell me, would you not also allow him entrance?

POLYGLOT INCANTATION

Siya ay nakatayo sa balikat ng bundok
She stands upon the mountain's shoulders
Langit ay kulay ng ginto at dugo
Sky's the color of gold and blood
Sumisigaw siya ¡Mira! ¡El sol!
See how the sun weeps
Tingnan mo! Umiiyak ang araw!
How this mountain slope burns
Nag-aapoy siya rin
Sky's the color of black pearls
Iyan lagi ang sa aking panaginip
This have I prophesied
Ang mukha ng araw ay umiiyak

And what are these glyphs
Wikang matemátiká
Some human machinery
Símbólo, enkantada, o gayuma
Maker of souls and tongues
Anong pisi o balat ng ahas
What twine or serpent skin binds
Silangan at kanluran
Pearl of the Orient
Este punto del embarco
Fractured archipelago
Ang mga anak mo ay nakakalat
Your children have scattered
Cielo el color de perlas negras
Do not forget that they have names
May sariling pangalan ang aming diwata

Hummingbird Diwata

Today the sun throws on his cloak of aquamarine plume, polishes his golden crown. Today he tires of courting the moon, fickle woman with so many suitors. So much song composed to call her down, there, where hawks perch and where the falcon's cry pierces the sleek blue gem of sky.

Today the sun descends and his aquamarine cloak becomes a field of violets, a handful of rubies. There are so many sweet flowers to soothe the hurt of the moon's constant thwarting. Even the sun tires of the chase. There are so many sweet flowers, and they open themselves like trumpets to show him their light, their own little moons of nectar. He pierces these fresh moons when he kisses. From his darting wings, his flitting tongue, poems to carry upon seawind and saltwind. Today, he promises them a salve of rain.

El Más Supremo

In the penthouse resides El Más Supremo, and none but the servants are allowed entrance into his suite. Barefoot, jangling brass anklets, they bring him the softest cloth and silks woven by virgins to drape upon his divans. Lazing about in linen robes, he gazes up at his ceiling, a clear dome filled with night sky. There in the stars, a tattooed prince, a many-headed beast slain by his hand. There, the string of pearls given to his princess. There, she waves away malevolent spirits by mimicking the ocean.

El Más Supremo sips chilled palm wine mixed with blue liqueur and the juice of calamansi, served in hollowed-out young coconut vessels. What meat has been scraped from inside of this shell, the chefs soak in this same azure cocktail, then sprinkle with sea salts and green sili.

What a banquet for El Más Supremo's eyes, these panorama sunsets the color of orchids, trees of the beloved orphan spirit swaying in guava-scented breezes. Processions from afar bring tithes from pearl farmers and miners of silver. Those who harvest rice fields also come to bring tribute. They do not stop to ask what he gives in return.

From above he cannot smell the salt of their bodies, nor can he see the lines carved into their brows. From above, the numerous are so very small.

MANILA MANGO

The Manila mango drips faster than my lips can catch it; in the manner of a Gauguin Tahitian portrait. The native girl with bare breasts points her eyes to the syphilitic man stealing her soul for art. "The bitch, she is," he could tell his shipmates, "when she refuses my advances." Another downcast look to her father, the chieftain, who moans when he sees her. The bitch, she is, for not coming home when she was told.

The sky is never gray and can't help but shrivel the fruit—if only there were some clouds to push out at it. But clouds would just dissolve in the ocean's glare. At least there's golden mango skin stretched over sweet flesh, honeying sap as it breaks.

Again, She Tells the First Story

Once, when there was no light, the wind danced with the sea, whose glassy surface became untamed funnels and silver-crested waves as she leapt and spun. The wind also spun and let out a mighty roar. You have heard this one before, no? How earth convulsed as if laughing. How seafloor forced her fingertips skyward. How she freed her body from the silent, murky depths.

She who was born of the rocks fell in love with the one who was born of sea spume. There upon the rocks, they spread seeds and soil, and from these the bamboo sprouted. It rooted itself in those rocks, and some say lightning, some say a bird split this bamboo open.

Others say a great serpent ruled the sea, and set upon his crown, a gleaming stone upon which the skyfolk spilled dark earth. I do not know why they tried to bury the serpent, but because of this, he hissed and lashed at them. The sea was once sweet and cool as rainwater. In the north, a medicine woman told us of her people's prayers for salt. Hot winds brought to them fragrances of the dead. After the waters receded, the shores became the color of clear crystals and blood.

Hija, I bring the sea tobacco leaves and fruit, but still no stories come to me. I plead with her, *O diwata, please accept this offering. O diwata, to hear your words is all I ask.* Today as ever, she gives me but silence.

UPLAND DANCE

hold arm taut kastoy

flat palm down kastoy

flick wrist so kastoy

ima pagay billít angin

step gong clang step

step trance chant step

clink bronze band clink

ima pagay billít angin

step plant bend step

step dip twirl step

tap wood click tap

ima pagay billít angin

step ripe earth step

step cut swirl step

thresh husk drum thresh

ima pagay billít angin

A Parable

The mermaid loosed her tongue against another, a twittering songbird in a fragrant tree. The mermaid loosed her tongue as if she were extending claws to swipe, as if craving warm blood. In her sleep, a vision. A tangle of thorns encircling the songbird. Doves' rank, rotted plumage. Maggot-infested eagles, wings and beaks, clipped. Lawin's crusty, milky eyes. Herons' open sores, overcome with infection.

Diwata came to the mermaid, stroked her thick, night-black hair. Do not fear, for one day the songbird will trill in a palace of pearls and summer seashells. And the mermaid breathed a sigh, lulled to sleep by the song of the ocean breeze.

Duyong 1

At midnight, the old men gather with oil lanterns aboard their fishing boats. This is when I feed. With rosaries in hand, they stab the water with machetes. Their sons say, "Do not be foolish. There are no more mermaids here. It is the crocodiles who are stealing our brothers."

Crocodiles! Ridiculous.

Crocodiles are not slick. My dolphin skin withstands the men's machetes. But make no mistake; the old men give me many scars.

From tangles of nets in the shallows, the old men cut me loose. They pray I may quickly find open sea. But do not think this is kindness.

As for their sons, their bodies come slipping deep into my home. Hands and feet, bound. Salvaged bodies full of soldiers' bullets, blooming blood flowers in my water. I sing them to sleep in my garden. If the old men only knew what care I take, bedding the sleeping sons of fishermen, warming their bodies in blankets of mud.

Duyong 2

You are the dreaming girl who walks outside of herself, into tidelands' star jasmine vine weaving, dripping sea spray. The air pulls your tiny feet, and you wiggle bare toes in the cool sand.

You are the rosy-faced girl who walks outside of herself. Tongues of moonlight penetrate banana leaf and coconut palm canopies. Chirping above you, dragonflies buzz and flit, deep magenta fire. Golden leafbirds and fairy bluebirds call you back to your father. You are the girl who does not heed her father's chirping messengers.

You listen to the story of branches, dipping their oversweet pink fruit into the swelling sea, touching smoothed wet stone. Wading waist-deep past the old men's boats, you tangle your mangrove fingers in the thick black ropes of your hair. You are the girl sloughing off dampened skin, blooming jade green, wild silken tendrils.

You remember your father's faint once upon a time. Something about danger. Something about the water who appears as a woman before you. She takes your hand, and your new skin ripens midnight violet. You are the girl whose new tail mimics a silver slicing razor.

DUYONG 3

I hear of men who love the sea cow. Pale skinned men, long delirious upon the balmy sea, they crawl ashore hungry, engorged. At the sight of them, she cries, and they think this is a siren song.

They ravish her stinking skin, her fleshy teats, with so many groping man hands and wet, open man mouths. One by one, they enter her body and spill so much seed. She cries, and with their spears, they slit her open and taste a feast of almond oil and sumptuous veal. She cries.

I am certain my song does not resemble hers.

Duyong 4

There is a man whose gods tell him to take the ocean as his consort. Carried in the womb of his lacquered palanquin, he arrives at his summer palace, laden with moonstone and pearl. His silk-spun robes of brocade lotus blossom drop upon the sand. He enters her.

And he waits. For many hours he waits.

I know this because I see his tender waterbird legs, his soft, hairy feet, pale and prune. The fool, how he treads, naked and flaccid, not knowing I am all around him, not knowing how close I come, and how I bare my claws. Oh, but how I resist swiping.

Instead, I sleep. I descend to my garden, and I sleep.

Into the dawn the man waits, and only his gods know what he expects to occur. Alone and shivering, he crawls ashore; he swears his attendants to secrecy.

Duyong 5

I am the daughter of a woman gathering seaweed pods. Against her husband's bidding, she wades too far into the bay, and a warm wave touches her belly. She wishes for it to caress her cheek. In a daydream, she closes her eyes, and the warm wave pulls at her shoulders. Slowly she submerges her swollen body, and this is how my mother's womb becomes the sea.

DRAGONFLIES

Behind the laughing house, the path is a sudden steep slide to the riverbank, and there are no stones along the path. Young ladies don't go to the river unchaperoned. Once, a young lady slid down the steep path and into the water. When she returned, her hair was a nest of mud and blue baby dragonflies. She tittered constantly, and touched her puckered lips with the tips of her wet fingers. She couldn't speak otherwise, fevered and whirring as she was. She stroked her throat and flicked her hair. She pulled open her thin blouse, and exposed her tiny breasts to the village boys. The handsome man in the laughing house stepped outside his door to see the commotion. Old church mothers clucked, "She shouldn't have been standing so close," as young boys learned to kick the dirt and crow. The man shook his head at them all. He covered this young lady's body with his white coat, placed a cold stethoscope against her burning skin, and found inside her heart the thrumming of the river.

There's a mermaid in the river behind the laughing house. She's the kind of mermaid who grabs at the ankles of young fishermen; the older ones' legs are too sturdy. She pulls the youngsters into the cool water. She slides her body against theirs. They too, surface, crowned with blue baby dragonflies and the river rushing inside their hearts. The old mothers clutch their rosary beads.

The river didn't used to be this close to the laughing house; one day, the river started to stretch itself wider and wider. The house started to throw stones, and cough up so much dust. Tickled by its own dust, it giggled and it shook. The goats knocked over trees with their hooves and the flat tops of their heads; they fed upon the roots until the trees all withered and the soil gave way underfoot. Even the dragonflies ate grass blades, one by one. The river, the house, the goats, the dragonflies, they did these things much to the old mothers' dismay, because the mermaid wanted to see the face of the godless, handsome man who lived inside the laughing house.

GARDEN

This is the story I was told: she doesn't remember when the yellow house was new, when the backyard, formerly a farmer's plot, was a mess of thorns and weeds. She doesn't remember when the first rains fell in autumn, when the weeds grew a grown-up's waist high. She doesn't remember how the soil was so rich, how the worms were so juicy, wriggling, and fat. She doesn't remember how the pechay just grew there, first tiny leaflings, delicate stalks. She doesn't remember, but the pechay grew hearty, its stalks thick and fibrous, leaves dark green and curly. She watched Mama pull those pechay right out of the earth; guisado, sinigang, nilaga bulalo.

This is what I remember: she cleared away the weeds and thorns, mulched and composted lemon tree branches. She helped lay down brick, and riverine pebbles. She dug up the earth, though decades had passed, the yellow house faded and painted anew. She dug up the earth, warm under her nails, still wriggling and juicy with worms. She planted tomatoes, parsley, and squash. She planted eggplant and yellow bell peppers. So long ago, Mama withered away, a skeleton, dementia-stricken. But she planted, and the tomatoes grew to her waist, beside deep pink rosebushes, blooming, full.

Estuary

Here, you seek solace, gliding in your vessel, sinew pulling skins taut over its cedar skeleton, the quickest blade slicing still water. Spear-fishing the silver current, your spine perpendicular to the cloudless sky. With the longest strokes, you surge into the river's mouth. For this, you know, there is no song.

Here, you coax the heat of your body into this cool water, and soon after, how salt crystallizes upon your shoulders. This quiet portent, slick, translucent sea kelp, patient buoys spilling tadpoles from their ruptured pods.

Here, you came on foot once, when you were a girl, weighted, breathing arid winds for days. Trudging through wild grasses and sage, whiptails scurrying about your ankles. You shivered in the cool night air until the glimmering and gleaming of water catching sun returned light to your lungs. Your hummingbird winged heart, and still such silence. Stepping upon the salt-lined shore, how the breeze tickled your face and hair. You scattered your father's ashes, dissipated his words. Some say you bathed in your father's ashes. Some say you breathed in his very words.

Here, no dragonflies accompany you, only the lean sound of you breaking the water's surface. This one song which only your body could compose.

JUNEAU

A wolf spirit has just passed; he roams beneath the dense cover of cedar and pine, onto the pebbled inlet shores. The wolf spirit calls, and fog lifts in the white of dawn. Baby orcas surface in sudden gusts of air, barely breaking the water's skin. The wolf spirit passes, a curl of fragrant smoke.

Estuary 2

She was born with fins and fishtail,
A quick blade slicing water.

She was her father's mermaid child,
A river demon, elders said.

She mimicked her cetaceous brothers,
Abalone diving bluest depths.

She polished smooth her brothers' masks,
Inlaid nacre half-moon eyes.

She lit oak pyres and bade the wind
A whispered requiem.

She knew the songs of tidal surge,
Of death-still moonless nights.

She veiled herself in cornflower
To soothe the ocean's rage.

She learned the language of the loom,
Mirrored grandmother's oak tree hands.

She spooled elk sinew pulled from bone,
Fleeting bodies, a meditation.

She carved spear tip and dagger hilt
In winter's shadowy corners.

She sharpened blades, and fled downriver
As elders clucked their tongues.

She emerged in spring, this tribe of one,
Hybrid coyote and cool green sea.

THE TRUE COLOR OF THE SEA

I.

sages' gardens, ginger root, and siren
glow of mist, green tongues of light
smoke and portents arousing hungers
magnolia-plumed gold moonstone heart
collecting rain in turtleshell hollows
of shoals and shelter, of stones that sing
of coral, of wine, of luminous unnamed

2.

cinnamon groves, veil of monsoon
moonless midnight's milky stars
the finest gold dust, tinder, mirror
of angels' tears, of devils' blood
of cooing doves, a child's fine bones
of sugarcane, and fistfuls of salt
of silk brocade, of laughter, of waiting

The Fire, Around Which We All Gather

I.

We bring her tobacco when she calls shrill bird trill carried upon air as though her voice were a body's warm rib cage we could wrap our arms around tight. We drop our weaving, we leave our kitchens. Elders once brought her tobacco rolled and bound with hemp; now we bring bulk carton Marlboros. Once, spirits fresh in glass jars; now Spanish brandy, limes, guava, and yams in baskets, salted fish in bundles. Now she is old but this firelight glows upon the face of a woman whose skin is sunned and taut; in her wide eyes we see sharp Lawin gaze, in her eyes we see sky. Her dancing wrist bones so delicate, as if fine fingers have known no field nor farmwork.

She has taken a blade to her own hair, once hung thick to her waistline, now falling in her eyes in jagged tresses, now exposing earlobes and neckline, her rough woven white blouse, its polished bone clasp undone, exposing one shoulder. She is young in the night's firelight though we dare not call her maiden. Our mothers say she snares others' husbands. Our grandmothers whisper her father a bird of prey. Our fathers lament she is the one they could not marry for she would not have them. She scoffed at offerings from the hunt, from the river, whose warm humid nights filled with serenade. Raising one index finger to her lips in a *shhh*, she confesses she has many times swooned to the verses of lovers under slivers of moon, ribbons of stars arranged into hunter and bow. Smoke curls from her lips, her eyes are closing, the diwata has arrived.

2.

Poet, yes. A conjurer of words, some have said, for I am the keeper of our words. I birth them and care for them, and when these words grow strong, a bridge. Just like that, a bridge. Those who come to listen to my stories, they fall into waking dream, hovering between the very earth upon which they stand, and the place where the spirits dwell.

Story, yes, for that is what poets make, story into song. We interpret what the birds say, what the spirits of the wind speak. They step into my dreams. They come to me in firelight, when I bathe in the river, and when I bed my lovers. They tell me things no human voice has spoken, secrets hidden in mountain caves, steel and blackened stone, the noise of machines. But the birds, yes, the birds, they tell me the sky.

And what of the sky, sighs the wind, for if not for me, you could not know her touch.

3.

And then she is the star maiden. And now she is the first woman, baring her breasts to feed a poisoned land. And he is the first man, father of black soil, bamboo blossom windstorm pestilence stone and confession. And she opens her body, the place from which all word grows. And he enters. And he enters. And he enters.

The whites of his eyes when he discovers she is a wolf, who is a woman, who is the prism in his throat. The immediacy. This wanting.

And from the wind's whirls we would call her silken breath, she brings a feast of word. Tree branches bend, she pulls them to her. And then she is a window, a vessel, a fork in the road, a fragrance lifting from tangerine skin. The rustle of a single page, the stillness of ocean before a typhoon. And then she is the fire, around which we all gather. And ever is she lover and beloved.

The whites of his eyes when he discovers she is a shark, who is a woman, who is his gravity. The immediacy. This wanting.

SEA INCANTATION

Sages' gardens, ginger root, siren
Glow of mist, jade tongues of light
Portents and smoke arousing hungers
Magnolia-plumed gold moonstone heart

Glow of mist, jade tongues of light
Collecting rain in turtleshell hollows
Magnolia-plumed gold moonstone heart
Shoals and shelter, stones that sing

Collecting rain in turtleshell hollows
Of coral, of wine, of luminous, unnamed
Souls and silted stones that singe
Of cinnamon groves' veil of monsoon

Of coral, of wine, of luminous, unnamed
Moonless midnight's milky stars
Cinnamon groves, veil of monsoon
The finest gold dust, tinder, mirror

Moonless midnight's milky stare
Of angels' tears and devils' blood
A vein of gold dust, tender marrow
Cooing doves, a child's fine bones

Angels tear and devils brood
Sugarcane, fistfuls of salt
My cooing dove, my child's fine bones
A silk brocade of laughter, waiting

Sugarcane, a fitful assault
Pretense and smoke arousing anger
A silk blockade of laughter, weighting
Cages, cordons, ginger root silence

EVE SPEAKS

Let the man who cannot dream be a condemned man. Who comes here but shadows of ourselves, where smoke seeps into plush velvet the color of lipstick and blood. This place is my dreamweaving, its iron sculptures, framed in light. Flickering chandeliers' fake fire. Still, wax melts and curls around my feet. The tables here are scratched brass, carved with names and regrets. You who regret, that is who you become. And you who need, but do not know why. Your need opens something in me which knows to anticipate dread. I anticipate your reprimand, and I anticipate your promise. Tell me then, as if I knew no words, tell me why you have created me to dread you.

Were I to assign us color, we would be mood ring, and then I would understand how heat and pressure make us glow bright crimson in our faux gold casing, how blood makes us murky aquamarine. Think of your pulse, beneath an undulating mirror of sky, think of salt crystallizing upon thighs and hands and lips, feathery seagrass tickling the soles of our feet. Even the coolest freshwater springs are momentary, dissipating. How moonless winters and sunrises can be held hostage, how nothing touches you. How this causes you to forget you are standing. How you are drowning. How you cannot feel your lungs. How the sky refuses to give its light to you. How you have forgotten how to breathe.

Tell me how your body sustains itself, how your rib cage is beyond bursting, how you still walk one foot in front of the next, how you count and name, count and name. How these words are still foreign sounds to you. How your skin still warms you, how your pupils still respond to movement. How you are a living shadow, a mountain echo. Tell me how you can possibly need, and how you can possibly need from me.

Were I to assign you color, you would be opaque, a fine slice of opal beneath the moon's veil. Were I to touch you, you'd shatter, and crumble into jasmine-scented powder. I would gather you beneath my fingernails, dust my love lines with you. Lover, I would break you. Lover, I will break you. Let there be the veil then, embroidered with dream flowers, petals resembling moths, serpents, leaves like clouds, unnameable desires. Let me always glance at empty doorways, knowing the movements beyond these are you drawing near.

Let this be the natural law—Lover, I will break you and compose a symphony with your bones. Of what remains, I shall grind into dust and mix with rain. Lover, do not come near, for I see story in your broken parts. Lover, do not promise, for when you do, I come to loathe words. Lover, do not speak, for what you say is vapor.

So here have I become the morning, and this is why water, and why jeweled skies, and why the night, and how silver makes song. Lover, did you not know I wrote my own creation story? Did you not know we all do.

THE BAMBOO'S INSOMNIA 2

Once upon a time, there was a seed, the tiniest speck in a dark sea of soil. But this seed did not know he was a seed; he was smaller than a fish eye. No light penetrated the dark soil, and so he broke himself open, and he stretched parts of himself into this soil, grabbed a hold of it and pushed himself upward. Lightbound, he pushed and grew into a tangle of eyes and hair and tendrils, thickening.

It occurred to him he had not yet learned to speak or to breathe. And so he grew himself into taut stalks, breaking soil, anticipating sky, while tendrils pulling water through his veins toughened him. He did not know his own name, but he knew rumors and dreams of air and mischievous birds.

This place before him was not a void but a crawl space, a tunnel he carved for himself inside his mother's body dying all around him. He broke right through her. He knew no other way.

There is no known portrait of her face, he now laments. Only my mosaic of many scattered stones.

CROSSING

Long, long ago, in the north, it was said the mountain opened herself to the people. A stream of the clearest water once flowed, there, where she provided shelter from windstorm and rain. The people of the mountain moved as shadows with their bows and spears through her forests. They gave thanks for she allowed them a crossing through her folds. Among these hunters, there was one who was blessed, for a diwata visited her.

In dreams, the diwata instructed her, and she instructed the others—with voices together, silver-winged birds trilling, then turning and curling like the mountain stream itself, it is said they sang songs of thanks and lament to the hunted, while in a stark vision, thunder and black smoke. In the sweet waters of the mountain stream, this stream she knew soon would rot, she cleaned antler, bone, and hoof as if she were bathing her own children. She adorned her robes and headdress, so that by firelight, she came to resemble these fallen animals. Then she called to the midnight sky.

I did not see this for myself, for this was many, many years before even my mother's mother was born. How tall the hunter woman stood, graced as she was. It is believed she crossed that bridge, the one between village and ancestors. She spoke words no one living could understand. She saw what no one living could see. Seas seized by great vessels, she said. Our men, huddled in the blindness of their hulls, bound.

Visitation

Often, she speaks of the one-eyed cat, natty-haired, gangly and gigantic. It visits her and corners her there, between the tomato patches and the rickety fence. It springs from the dirt and into the lemon trees' boughs. It stares with its one milky eye. It yowls like no creature she has ever known.

As its wailing body finally disappears with the wind, news arrives of a loved one's departing soul. An elder succumbing to illness, an accident in the fields, flesh sliced and broken by so many rusted blades, invading armies' guns and gasoline.

The harvest became an offering to the war gods. Young women, roped and gagged. Many times, it happens like this. From fruit trees' branches or curled about her ankles, the cat stares through her with its milky eye. Its other eye, half scab, half absence, stares at her too. Then the tragedy.

"Your death will come with fire," she weeps to her robust grandfather, and without speaking, he places around her neck his silver amulet—Saint Michael sashed in silk with glinting sword. The following day, uniformed men come out of the jungle, the trees behind them in flames.

Tugging at his shirt and forcing words between sobs and frantic breaths, she knows her father will not hear. Unfaithed by city whores, and nursing cheap gin, he still suspects his own father's spirit will make visitation upon him. A wisp of old man floating at the foot of the bed, blessing the blisters of his feet with touch.

Call It Talisman (If You Must)

I.

Here, the blind old man tapped this marking into my left arm and breastbone. He used his tapping stick and his sharpened irons. These are leaves and grass blades. These are sunbursts of flower petals, the flitting eyes of moth wings and cicadas. This here, the seer and her seeing stones. The glass eye with which she viewed the heavens. Above her mountain village, the stars arranged into hunter and bow, arrow aimed at mighty Lawin.

This is not thunder. No, only men are marked with thunder. He marked my flesh with the swirls of our village stream. Here, on my right shoulder. What I see is no stream, but a blade which women conceal beneath their skirts. Even today, we do this, though it is not proper, the elders say, for women to be marked for war.

It is no secret. Women did indeed fight alongside the men once. Few talk about it these days. The black-robed holy men, who carried more curses than prayer, so feared armed women, they branded us savage and sinful, they called us monsters. Women who tucked skirts between their legs, tongues of knives, hands like tilling tools, we returned home to nurse our babies after washing clean our bloodied hands.

2.

No, daughter, these are no talismans upon my flesh. The blind old man wished to give me markings in the patterns of my father's fields, for he walked my father's lands, from new growth's edges to the greenest center, every sunrise in wordless prayer. Many years, he did this, never once opening his eyes. But by the time I grew old enough to marry, all his fields my father lost to the fire, and to the papers of the wealthy, not of this land but of gray cities far away from here.

He marked my flesh with the swirls of our village stream, though its cool, sweet water, its bubbling, no longer gives us music. It has long since been fenced and dammed, but by whom, no one who ever shows himself. Its music we have all of us forgotten. And the flowering trees that once dipped its branches into the water to drink have all withered. There is no sense in my very body carrying a reminder of all that is lost to us, for no healer of scars, and no magical markings could save any of it. This is no stream, no. It is the curve of a warrior blade.

3.

This is how my flesh was marked with the ash of burnt coconut husk and sugarcane, so that I could marry. But all the young men had neither land nor wealth, and invading armies came with bayonets. Sun worshippers, harboring no love for things of this land.

When my grandfather's father was still a young man, an army of pale men came to our forest. But our men took their heads with ease. Running dogs, whimpering, they were cowards. And even the lowlanders, some marked with the talismans of their own elders, some who had grown their hair down to their waistlines, hid in our forests with rifles and the sharpest knives. They fought those pale men for many years, until those white ghosts numbered so few, they boarded their steamships and they fled.

But these sun worshippers, they were cruel. They used the young women as whores, slid loaded pistols between their legs, gave them sores and fevers which none of our medicines could cure. The sun worshippers also took heads, but left these to rot where they fell. No hunters were these, but mercenaries, beasts. This is why the sun wept a sky the color of black pearls. This is why he weeps still.

4.

He took me, from the river's edge, where I washed clothes for the church man's daughter. He took me, gripped between his fists. I feared that if I tried to escape, I would fall, pierced by the sharpest bayonet. I knew for sure I would bleed, for I had lived my entire life in my father's house and had never before touched man. When the soldier came with his vulgar words, I leaned farther over the edge than I should have. But so venomous, his words. Upon the banks of the river for which my father was named, there, the soldier took me and took me, and the river could do nothing. I knew my brothers too could do nothing. There, he tore me in two.

My child, your father's eyes. My child, one day you will curse his name.

A Little Bit About Lola Ilang

During the war, the old women would still go outside the house to smoke their hand-rolled tobacco after cleaning the suppertime dishes. But so the Japanese soldiers would not see them, they learned to flip their cigarettes with the lit ends inside their mouths. They flipped their cigarettes with their tongues so fast, and we kids would try to copy them. We burned our own tongues trying. Lola Ilang used to do this, and I tried to copy her. It hurt! It hurt so much when I burned my tongue! Yes, Lola Ilang used to cook the best pochero, and foreigners thought it was a little weird, to cook banana with bok choy. You use the saba banana. No other kind is sweet enough. Do you know, when she died, everyone had already forgotten how old she was? We asked her some years ago, and even she had forgotten. But I was saying about the war. No, the women did not want the soldiers to find them. You know what the soldiers did to the women here. The Japanese buried so much gold in our hills. This is because our northernmost provinces were the last places they set foot before their ships left, after their emperor surrendered. They stole this gold, Spanish gold, from our churches. You know, not too long ago, some of the Japanese who had gone into hiding were found in the hills. They were so old. They never knew how the war ended.

PANANAGHOY

Ay, ay!

Bodies disassembled in church courtyards, mango blossom boughs knotted, hewn from roots with dull blades. The moon was blood, and sometimes she'd close her eyes. Sometimes so much poetry, prayers on the parched lips of dying men, forced her to hide. Even the barest trees were always good for hiding, and solitary herons' wings swift slicing through cloud. How they'd lacerate sky, and how sky bled, bending in arcs and wisps after the bombs fell. The stillness terrified us all. And those very veiled women who prayed with rose-scented rosaries opened their legs for so little rice and fish. Yes, this, I saw. And with my own eyes, this I see still.

Ay, ay!

Pasig

The spirits no longer bathe here, though in moonlight, my eyes trick me sometimes, and I think it is the weeping tree I see, seducing dream-filled dissidents. Their young bloated bodies sleep in the riverbed and greet me as they surface.

Tell me, why would the diwata visit this dead, filthy place, to make a home among its broken things, to drink its filthy water, to breathe its acrid air?

No, there is no more reason for her to return. We may as well fill it with mud and forget, for there is nothing but wordless burial here. And no one who will say grace.

How I No Longer Believe in Pious Women

I am certain something tawdry, a craving for stiletto-heeled patent leather, perfume of tiger lilies and tobacco, swigs from the whiskey bottle, leaving rings of whore-red lipstick, evidence of the carnal slithers beneath pink skin. I am certain their forked tongues press hard against their palates so that strings of profanity remain caged, a virgin's thighs shut tight. I am certain that rough neighborhoods' wafting aromas, sticky nightclubs of glittery G-stringed putas, of gold-toothed criminals with teardrop tattoos make their hearts flutter, curl their hands into manicured talons, move their tongues to lick shiny bicuspids. All the while, their lips pursed in feigned disdain. I do not believe in pious women, but the red imprints of corset, pale lace, and garter upon breathing, hot flesh.

Oh, but how I have strayed. From my story, how I have strayed.

SHE LAMENTS UNNUMBERED LOSSES

What things I have cast into the sea I have done this in order to forget my child if not for this you would curse your fathers their names their fists smother my every cry I have done this in order to forget my child the villagers tell me this is for the best their names their fists smother my every cry our medicine woman's hands and tongue severed the villagers tell me this is for the best both age and fire have blinded her our medicine woman's hands and tongue severed the air is rank with the fragrance of death both age and fire have blinded her my own mother has cast me away the air is rank with the fragrance of death I have bled and so I am impure my own mother has cast me away oh Holy Mary oh Mother of God I have bled and so I am impure pray for us sinners take me into your folds oh Holy Mary oh Mother of God the priests tell me I may yet be saved pray for us sinners take me into your folds under night's cover they creep into my bed the priests tell me I may yet be saved they say in God's name this is for the best under night's cover they creep into my bed they teach me to pray force me onto my knees they say in God's name this is for the best they tell me I am going to heaven they teach me to pray force me onto my knees I want to believe them I want to be saved they tell me I am going to heaven if not for this you would curse your fathers I want to believe them I want to be saved what things I have cast into the sea

A Chorus of Villagers Sing a Song from another Time Now Only a Memory

Come back, return! It is not yet the time to wander,
Come back, return! It is not yet the time to wander.

When it is your hour, then you will be called,
When it is your hour, then you will be called.

Come back to the village, return to the mountain—
Her trees invite you to climb into their arms!

Come back to the mountain, return to the stream—
Its musical bubbling, its sweet and cool waters!

Come back to the stream, return to the fishponds—
The fish are swimming in silvery streaks!

Come back to the village, return to your home—
Your children await the softest lullaby!

Come back, return! It is not yet the time to wander,
When it is your time, then you will be called.

THE VILLAGERS SING OF THE WOMAN WHO BECOMES A WAVE WHO BECOMES THE WATER WHO BECOMES THE WIND

she weaves words into the fabric of sky
she knows the stars, an ascension of pearls
she is witness, keeper of starlight
she weeps silver tears when the moon is full

she knows the stars, an ascension of pearls
she is mother, the deepest ocean
she weeps silver tears when the moon is full
leaf storm, rice terrace, color of midnight

she is mother, the deepest ocean
sunrise, black pearl, blood, and serpent
leaf storm, rice terrace, color of midnight
leaping, spinning, fingertips skyward

sunrise, black pearl, blood and serpent
with tobacco and fruit to appease the silence
leaping, spinning, fingertips skyward
she is a silver-winged bird in flight

with tobacco and fruit to appease the silence
the medicine woman prays for salt
she is a silver-winged bird in flight
she has marked her own flesh with thunder

the medicine woman prays for salt
riverbed fragrance, night herons diving
she has marked her own flesh with thunder
here, the curve of a warrior blade

riverbed fragrance, night herons diving
she is witness, keeper of starlight
here, the curve of a warrior blade
she weaves words into the fabric of sky

Eve Speaks 2

One by one the stars go out, and I wonder how you will navigate to this place where I am standing. To some, this would be cause for prayer, though I have never known how to pray. Sad little pocket of silence here, where my shadow no longer resembles me. Here, within my dreamweaving, it is always autumn, and old men and trannies dance to the feedback and treble of someone else's distant music. The walls spill their electrical wire and fuse boxes, and one by one the stars go out. Each dying flicker there, and the oars of your boatmen grow silent. Swishing water against hulls become a whisper. I watch these wordless deaths, I light a beacon, and let the oarsmen resume their song.

Come ashore, my winsome pilgrim, kiss the earth if you must. See how this collection of stolen bones becomes a wolf. Place your open hand there, and the delicate skin of your wrist supine, so that she may know your scent. Within salt circles, unlock this cage of skin with a hairpin. See the flesh burn away, until all that remains is the seashell. Place your ear gently against her heart, a memory of ocean. Take a lock of her hair; bind it with silk. Do not speak your intention. Bury it beneath the most fragrant tree in this garden, and remember to taste the wind. Dear pilgrim, now there is cause for prayer, even for one who has forgotten the words.

In the City, a New Congregation Finds Her

She keeps safe our memory when nothing's committed to stone.
Sibilant selvedge woman, thread and knots talkstory woman.

She whose memories not paperbound, lover of midnight words.
Scrawled myth upon flesh woman, indigo testimony tattoo woman.

We bring her spirits we've captured in bottles.
Firewater woman, imbibes the spirits woman.

We bring her dried tobacco leaves and tea.
Exhales the word woman, full-moon weaving woman.

She looses her thick hair from its pins and coils.
Litany liturgy woman, stitching suture woman.

She settles into her favorite chair, she always begins like this.
Soul-gatherer woman, spiderweb songbird woman.

She breathes steam from tea, steeped stems and petals.
Piece and patchwork woman, down-home cookin' woman.

She crushes anise stars, sweetens nightmare into reverie.
Stone by stone woman, singed and soot woman.

She cups glazed clay between cracked hands.
Silver-winged bird woman, riverine dream-filled woman.

She rubs together palms callused, she who conjures for us a feast.
Sugar tinctured moonwoman, twittering songstress moonwoman.

She whose eyes widen with black thundercloud and sea.
Salt luster sirenwoman, winter solstice madwoman.

She whose voice billows and peals, she whose eyes gaze nowhere.
Howling nomad madwoman, cut the bullshit madwoman.

Her lips release language not of paper sometimes (we think) she forgets.
Older than the ocean woman, sargassum and seashell woman.

She who has kept vigil always, she of the wing-kissed sunset.
Sipping starlight woman, before there was a nailed god woman.

Eve's Aubade

Let rainbows arc and sprout from the base of my tongue and into your cupped palms, before the saltwater fishponds teem quicksilver, deep blue, and sunrise hues, before the aqueducts and irrigation ditches are sculpted into damp earth, before these mango groves are hewn, before these gravel paths ripen with fallen fruit. Before we part, breathe your song into me.

Remain by my side as wind deity, as word, as eyes bright with both dusk and amber. Remain with me so that we may keep vigil, both of us before morning's honeyed light filters through fire escapes. In our vigil, let there be only witness, and I will offer you stillness rising into unfettered dawn. Here I will weave a dreaming of lovemaking bodies' fire and salt. Here, I will teach your hands to weave crescent moon into ocean current, serpent hiss into river's rush. Here I shall weave a selvedge of we.

Ever shall there be a we, a ceaseless, insistent we, the fiercest we, bound only to the knowledge of scars upon my flesh, and the segment of my spine which aches to sprout wings. Deep within lightless dovecotes, this we shall remember the lamentation of songbirds as it remembers the lingering warmth of your retreating form. Ever shall this we know how tender, your flesh at the throat, how your fecund black loam scent sates me.

Do not let the sun steal you from my side and set you wandering, for now we know red hibiscus blooms here in your city of constant sirens. Bring me your bones and your fire, and I will keep them safe.

HAVING BEEN CAST, EVE IMPLORES

I want to know the fires your hands bring—
the fractured fates and deep-set furious lives,
the weaving of your heart lines, and how perched
upon the finest blade of language, the verses
you have breathed into your city of constant sirens.

I want to know the words to your prayer—
my earliest memory, a thirst for your bones.
Tell me what you know of redemption, dear one,
and blossoms of hope unfurling their first petals.
Tell me you awaken holding my name in your hands.

I want to know the scent of your promise—
an azure calm that rises and falls, your lungs
drawing air, whispering. Muse, Diwata,
I am your constant siren, your ocean lullaby.
Diwata, I am your midnight dragonfly song.

Having Been Cast, Eve Implores 2

Dear Night Sky, dear Veil, hear me. A lullaby aches in my rib cage. Today, I am a dovecote, and there are songbirds cooing inside, twittering, goldened, precious. How they all at once alight as I open my body to your waning autumn moon. I am waiting for you to fill me.

Dear Wounded One, I dream you are fading, though you are not lost to me. The starlight of your bones still pulls me to you, to your pieces of worship, to the work of your hands. I still know the whisper of your scarring fissures; I know these are calling to me.

Dear Impossible Song, dear Vesper Song, you wander along the sun's path, its lowest point, this longest night. I know this, the music of your promise. And still I hope implausibly, for today, my body is an earthen bowl to be filled, and to be filled again.

MEDICINE SONG

windstorm in the throat, burning

hummingbird in the throat, flying

river tide in the throat, howling

eagle in the throat, blessing

birch tree in the lungs, branching

thundercloud in the lungs, singing

buffalo in the lungs, rumbling

she-wolf in the lungs, leaping

voice that is the smoke, weaving

voice that is the fox, laughing

voice that is coyote, thrumming

voice that is the drum, praying

WHY GIRLS DO NOT SPEAK

You are wondering why some girls have lost their voices, when this one here rushes her words as if she were a brook, engorged with monsoon. At the running waters of Agos, a girl once stopped to fill her canteen. She had come down from Bundok with her father's ashes. Because her father had no sons, an unusual occurrence, the task came upon her to scatter his ashes into Dagat, which the lowlanders called El Mar.

As I have said, it was unusual for the men of Bundok not to father any sons. If one woman into whom he planted his seed could not give him one son, the man would simply plant his seed into a different woman. And if she could not give him a son, he would continue planting his seed into other women until a son resulted. Many girl children were born this way, set aside by their fathers.

But her father was different. He loved his child and he could not bear to cast her away. He cropped her hair to her skull, and taught her to hunt. Like a man, she learned to spear fish, to build bangka, to chisel their deities in wood. She kept vigil with the other hunters, and yes, she also took heads. She came to tell stories of the hunt, and the people loved her stories best. Few knew this young storyteller was a girl.

Now, regarding the girl children of Bundok, pale men from the coastal lowlands came to Bundok. They had heard stories of the women far outnumbering the men. They came and found so many fatherless daughters, weaving mats, dyeing cloth, cooking meals, learning to tell story. Some sat idle, somber, bored, for there were more girls than needed to perform all of the daily work. When the elders explained to the pale men there were not enough of their own men to marry all of these young women, the pale men promised to supply many good husbands. To this, the elders responded with relief.

What the pale men did not tell the elders is that they forbade their women from stepping outdoors lest the sun darken them. The pale men forced their women's once bare feet into narrow, pinching shoes, shut their women inside exquisite whalebone cages, which broke the wives' ribs, and which did not allow them to draw air. Faint, the wives could no longer sing. They lost their ability to speak. Those wives who were still able to utter few words the pale men beat properly, as their fathers and mothers had taught them, as they would teach their sons and daughters. The wives learned silence was their only shield. When our young storyteller arrived with her father's ashes at Dagat, she begged the wives to return with her, but they claimed they did not recognize her, and so she returned to Bundok alone.

TOCAYA

Madre, ¿por qué cuando se corre una estrella o luce un relámpago se dice:

Santa Bárbara bendita,
que en el cielo estás escrita
con papel y agua bendita?

—Federico García Lorca, *La Casa de Bernarda Alba*

Patron saint of lightning bolts

you, of sharpened tongue,

maiden of thunder and war,

guard us against malediction.

Beautiful girl, seer, mártir,

poeta, rebel, tattooed daughter.

Our lady of gunpowder,

our lady of bullets,

our lady of men deep in the earth.

Sweet anise star, bold pomegranate,

saint of machete, two spirit bull.

ASWANG

I am the dark-hued bitch; see how wide my maw, my bloodmoon eyes,
And by daylight, see the tangles and knots of my riverine hair.
I am the bad daughter, the freedom fighter, the shaper of death masks.
I am the snake, I am the crone; I am caretaker of these ancient trees.
I am the winged tik-tik, tik-tik, tik-tik, tik-tik; I am close,
And from under the floorboards, the grunting black pig,
Cool in the dirt, mushrooms between my toes, I wait.
I am the encroaching wilderness, the bowels of these mountains.
I am the opposite of your blessed womb; I am your inverted mirror.
Guard your unborn children, burn me with your seed and salt,
Upend me, bend my body, cleave me beyond function. Blame me.

NOTES

"The Bamboo's Insomnia" was written after Eduardo Galeano's "Night/I," from *Book of Embraces* (Norton).

"Manila Mango" was written after Susanna Kittredge's "Sequitur."

"Upland Dance" was written after the Ifugao Music and Dance Ensemble of Banaue San Francisco performance, September 2007. The words *ima*, *pagay*, *billit*, and *angin* are Ilocano words meaning "hand," "rice plant," "bird," and "wind." *Kastoy* means "like this."

"Duyong I" uses "salvaged" in the term's Philippine context. Poet and journalist Jose F. Lacaba writes, "As used in the Philippines, the verb 'salvage' and the noun 'salvaging' are the slang equivalents of the terms 'to execute extrajudicially, to assassinate' and 'extrajudicial execution,' terms used by human-rights organizations such as Amnesty International."

"Call It Talisman (If You Must)" was inspired by the indigenous tattoo revival of the Tatak ng Apat na Alon Tribe, and anthropologist Ikin Salvador's "Signs on Skin: Beauty and Being: Traditional Tattoos and Tooth Blackening among the Philippine Cordillera" exhibit and talk at Pusod in Berkeley, October 2004. In one photograph, a group of newly tattooed, young Ilubo warriors posed in traditional headdresses and loincloths for a portrait in 1949. Their rite of passage (for which they were inked) was the killing of invading Japanese soldiers. The Ilubo were traditionally headhunters.

"Eve Speaks 2" borrows the line "One by one the stars go out" from Tu Fu's "A Restless Night in Camp."

"Having Been Cast, Eve Implores 2" was written after Jennifer K. Sweeney's *Salt Memory* (Main Street Rag).

"Medicine Song" was written after the All Nations Drum Group performance at UC Berkeley's 2009 Flor y Canto.

"Aswang" was written after Rachelle Cruz's currently unpublished poetry collection, *Ascela at the World's Greatest Fair*, and Vince Gotera's "Aswang." Anthropologist Alicia Magos has written that in an effort to spread Catholicism in the Philippines, the early Spanish Catholic clerics maligned the "pagan and demonic" indigenous women priests by calling them Aswang, a god of evil. "It was a perfect religious-military tool for conquering other cultures. Through time, the term *aswang* was invented and its description became more morbid and cruel as generations passed these fabricated stories." The *aswang* is now known as a mythical creature that uses her long, thin tongue to suck babies out of their mothers' wombs.

Acknowledgments

Thank you to the editors of the following publications in which some of these poems have previously appeared, some in earlier versions: *2nd Avenue Poetry, Action Yes, Amerarcana, Boxcar Poetry Review, Crate, The Drunken Boat, Fairy Tale Review, In Our Own Words, In the Grove, MiPOesias, New American Writing, Notre Dame Review, Octopus Magazine, Pacific Review, Poets & Artists, Tinfish, Versal, Womb Poetry, Word Riot, XCP: Cross Cultural Poetics, Zoland Poetry,* and in the anthology *Field of Mirrors* (San Francisco: PAWA, Inc., 2008).

Thank you to my husband and partner Oscar Bermeo. Thank you Maxine Chernoff, Stacy Doris, and Jaime Jacinto; to Francisco Aragón, Tara Betts, Peter Conners, Rigoberto González, Wayne Hangad, Lee Herrick, Javier O. Huerta, Craig Santos Perez, Jennifer Reimer, Matthew Shenoda, Evie Shockley, Stephen Hong Sohn, Truong Tran, Sunny Vergara, Rich Villar, Thom Ward, and Bryan Thao Worra. *Salamat at Dios ti Agngina* to Gina Apostol, Rick Barot, Terry Bautista, Vangie Buell, Nick Carbó, Rachelle Cruz, Oliver de la Paz, M. Evelina Galang, Sarah Gambito, Vince Gotera, Luisa Igloria, Paolo Javier, Joseph O. Legaspi, Edwin A. Lozada, Rebecca Mabanglo-Mayor, Aimee Nezhukumatathil, Jon Pineda, Bino A. Realuyo, Al Robles (RIP), Tony Robles, Patrick Rosal, Anthem Salgado, Lara Stapleton, Leny Mendoza Strobel, Eileen R. Tabios, Jean Vengua, and Marianne Villanueva.

About the Author

Barbara Jane Reyes was born in Manila, Philippines, and raised in the San Francisco Bay Area. She received her BA in Ethnic Studies at UC Berkeley, and her MFA at San Francisco State University. She is the author of *Gravities of Center* (Arkipelago, 2003), and *Poeta en San Francisco* (Tinfish, 2005), which received the James Laughlin Award of the Academy of American Poets. She has taught Creative Writing at Mills College and Philippine Studies at University of San Francisco. She lives with her husband, poet Oscar Bermeo, in Oakland.

BOA Editions, Ltd.
American Poets Continuum Series

Colophon

Diwata, poems by Barbara Jane Reyes, is set in Centaur, a digitalized version of the font designed for Monotype by Bruce Rogers in 1928. The italic, based on drawings by Frederic Warde, is an interpretation of the work of the sixteenth-century printer and calligrapher Ludovico degli Arrighi, after whom it is named. The display type is Sackers Gothic.

The publication of this book is made possible, in part, by the special support of the following individuals:

Anonymous
Gwen & Gary Conners
Mark & Karen Conners
Charles & Barbara Coté in memory of Charlie Coté Jr.
Robert L. Giron
Kip & Debby Hale
Janice N. Harrington & Robert Dale Parker
G. Jean Howard
Bob & Willy Hursh
Robin, Hollon & Casey Hursh in memory of Peter Hursh
X. J. & Dorothy M. Kennedy
John & Barbara Lovenheim
Elissa & Ernie Orlando
Boo Poulin
Deborah Ronnen & Sherman Levey
Steven O. Russell & Phyllis Rifkin-Russell
Vicki & Richard Schwartz
Evie Shockley in memory of Lucille Clifton
Ellen Wallack
Pat & Mike Wilder
Glenn & Helen William